"Indy Neogy effectively addresses the nuan~~ ~~
analysis and awareness, offerin
suggestions for understanding th
plays in internal and external bus
recommend this guide for those i
ever-evolving cultural communicat   ~~...~~ges of globalisation."

"Awareness and authenticity are at the heart of effective cross-cultural communication. This succinct guide captures the key principles you need to succeed. It provides clarity, actionable guidance and inspiration to better navigate cross-cultural communication in our increasingly interconnected world of business."

"Neogy provides a useful roadmap through the pitfalls and opportunities of cross-cultural, global communication. Highly relevant and accessible, key points like authenticity, inclusion, and self-awareness are explained in a navigable manner that will resonate with marketers and managers alike."

"Brisk but not superficial, this guide is a good introduction to the pitfalls and opportunities open to organisations seeking a global presence. Neogy offers a great mix of theory, practice, stories, and advice."

"A concise, yet detailed, manual on the paramount importance of cross-cultural communications in a globalised world. This is the book that should be read, analysed and implemented by all members of an organisation, regardless of how long they have been with the company, or what position they hold."

SKAISTE SRUOGAITE, EXTERNAL RELATIONS MANAGER – PROCTOR & GAMBLE

"Culture matters in international business. This books breaks down the 30 plus years of research on this topic to give anyone from CEOs to new hires a snapshot of how to work more effectively in a culturally sensitive environment."

ATHENA D'AMATO, DIRECTOR OF OPERATIONS – ANGLE MEDIA GROUP

"Peeling back the onion of complex culture clash has never been so easy or tearless. Reading this guide will prevent getting lost in translation and enhance cross-cultural competence. Two soles up, except in Thailand and Iraq!"

RANDY TINKERMAN, INTERNATIONAL WIND PIONEER – DEUTSCHE WINDGUARD

WHEN CULTURE MATTERS

THE 55-MINUTE GUIDE TO BETTER
CROSS-CULTURAL COMMUNICATION
BY **INDY NEOGY**

CHAIN OF CUSTODY

ALL BOOKS IN THE 55-MINUTE GUIDE SERIES ARE PRINT ON DEMAND (POD), A MODEL
OFFERING SIGNIFICANT ENVIRONMENTAL ADVANTAGES OVER TRADITIONAL OFFSET
PRINTING. THE PRINTER OF THIS BOOK, LIGHTNING SOURCE®, IS CHAIN OF CUSTODY
(COC) CERTIFIED BY THE FOREST STEWARDSHIP COUNCIL™ (FSC®), THE PROGRAMME
FOR THE ENDORSEMENT OF FOREST CERTIFICATION™ (PEFC™), AND THE SUSTAINABLE
FORESTRY INITIATIVE® (SFI®), ENSURING THE INTEGRITY OF THE PAPER SUPPLY CHAIN
AND THAT THE PAPER USED IN PRINTING THIS BOOK IS FROM RESPONSIBLY MANAGED
FORESTS.

FIRST PUBLISHED IN 2012 BY

VERB PUBLISHING LTD
THE COW SHED, HYDE HALL FARM,
BUCKLAND, HERTS SG9 0RU,
UNITED KINGDOM

ISBN 978-0-9564672-5-6

TO MY PARENTS. THEIR MARRIAGE ACROSS CULTURES WAS MY FORMATIVE EXPERIENCE OF CROSS-CULTURAL COMMUNICATION.

WHAT'S INSIDE

In today's global economy, what international business leaders are continually cracking their shins against is culture.

1. INTRODUCTION

WHAT THIS BOOK'S ABOUT

Everyone talks about globalisation these days – and what it means for where and how people live their lives, what they eat, how they dress. The impact of a truly global economy is still being unravelled by economists, politicians and pundits.

For business people, globalisation means who you source from, work with and sell to may be changing dramatically. A single supply chain can cross myriad national borders. But few business leaders feel at ease with the challenge of doing business internationally.

What they continually crack their shins against is CULTURE. It changes from place to place, it can't be ignored, and it won't go away. That's why this book aims to provide a whistle-stop tour of the CULTURAL DIMENSION OF INTERNATIONAL BUSINESS – what it is, why it matters, and what business leaders can do better to address it.

At the crux of the problem of culture in business is COMMUNICATION. Hence the subtitle. I've written this book for anyone from CEOs to the newest, most junior recruit in a department doing business across borders.

The goal of this book is to show you why culture matters in international business, and how you can manage it better.

I'd like to inspire you to make cross-cultural understanding PART OF HOW YOU CONDUCT BUSINESS COMMUNICATIONS. To do that, I've boiled down cross-cultural communication so it's a concept you can digest in under an hour (no mean feat, given 30+ years of research in this field!). You'll also need PRACTICAL TIPS about what you can do as a leader in business, and as a participant in cross-cultural conversations. Finally, we'll look at the FUTURE OF CROSS-CULTURAL COMMUNICATIONS.

All the clashes and misunderstandings you currently experience are likely to intensify as the world grows ever more inter-connected. By the end of the book, you should have a stronger appetite and some new ideas to begin wrestling with some pretty tricky situations including:

→ International marketing
→ Global conduct
→ Communications in groups
→ 1:1 conversations
→ Negotiating across cultures

On every facing page you'll find a summary of core thoughts and ideas. Try adding them to presentations or the bottom of your emails and see if you can start a conversation.

HOW IT'S STRUCTURED

→   First, we explore the basics — what we mean by the words CULTURE and COMMUNICATION.

→   Second, we look at the three dimensions of communication that matter most in business. International, group and individual communication each get a chapter.

→   Third, we delve into applying this knowledge in practice.

→   Fourth, the afterword offers a glimpse into the future, identifying what matters most and where you can look for more help.

As with all 55-MINUTE GUIDES, you'll find a glossary at the back to help align our understandings of the main terms. And, as we wend our way through the book, key points will be spotlighted on the even-numbered pages.

FAST CULTURE = **fads and fashions**

SLOW CULTURE = **deeper trends**

VERY SLOW CULTURE = **values underlying 'culture-clash'**

2. CULTURE – IT'S A LOT LIKE GRAVITY

DEFINING CULTURE

Like gravity in the physical world, culture is easiest to define by its effects. Geert Hofstede is the culture researcher best known in the business world. He defined culture as, "the collective mental programming of the people in an environment." Culture is a characteristic of GROUPS, NOT INDIVIDUALS. It is a prism through which people interpret events and decide actions.

Grant McCracken, in his book CHIEF CULTURE OFFICER, deals mainly with the symbols and meanings of popular culture. He introduces a useful notion of FAST AND SLOW CULTURE which, for him, separates the fads and fashions of the moment from slower cultural changes relating to deeper themes in life. I'd like to extend this and add the category VERY SLOW CULTURE, which is composed of the values that underlie many international culture-clashes.

Hofstede also produced a famous model of culture that has become a cliché, but it's too useful to reinvent – THE ONION. The innermost layer is VALUES, which change very slowly. In the roughly 40 years since Hofstede undertook his first study, repeated studies have not shown a great deal of change in cultural values of countries around the world. Values underlie

Hofstede's Onion, a famous model of culture:

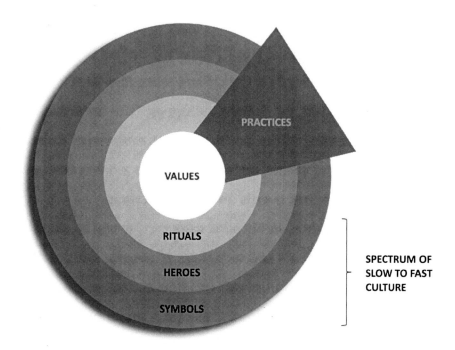

ATTITUDES AND RULES in a society. Next are successive layers of RITUALS, HEROES AND SYMBOLS, each of which shifts more easily than the last. These three layers are EXPRESSIONS OF THE VALUES analogous to McCracken's spectrum of SLOW TO FAST CULTURE. Two key points:

→ CULTURE IS LARGELY AN UNCONSCIOUS INFLUENCE ON PEOPLE. There's a cliché of culture as an iceberg – 90% is underwater. Expressions (language, dress, symbols and rituals) obviously differ, but the deeper differences in values and beliefs are usually unspoken. Culture is the sea fish swim in – until you move out of it, many features are invisible. Hence the need to actively seek awareness.

→ BEHAVIOUR IS A PRODUCT OF CULTURE AND INDIVIDUAL TRAITS, COMBINED WITH CONTEXT OF THE MOMENT. So culture is a simple lens to apply to communications with larger groups, but requires extra thought when applied to individuals.

Culture exists at MANY LEVELS – groups, departments, professions, regions, countries and more. In business, two main areas require attention:

→ ORGANISATIONAL CULTURE – the culture of a company (and the sub-cultures inside that).

Communication requires a shared system of signs and semiotic rules. If you don't know the semaphore code, all you'll see is flags waving!

→ INTERNATIONAL CULTURE – the cultures of groups of people from different parts of the world.

For this book we're going to concentrate on international culture – because we've only got 53 minutes now and globalisation is a pressing fact for most businesses. It also provides a rich pool of examples for thinking about culture in general – maybe it's the easiest 'culture-clash' to grasp.

DEFINING COMMUNICATION

Communication is a process where information is transferred from one entity to another. However different they are, they must share what the academics call a REPERTOIRE OF SIGNS AND SEMIOTIC RULES. Without sharing that system, it's hard for the receiver to make sense of the sender's signals. However, in the vast majority of business communication, the information transfer is undertaken in order to influence the actions of the other party. Rarely will a business simply communicate facts. WE INTEND TO INFLUENCE THEIR PATH OF ACTION.

Let's flip this point about influence on its head. If the point of business communication is to convey information and influence others, then ANYTHING THE COMPANY DOES THAT INFLUENCES PEOPLE (FOR BETTER OR WORSE) IS COMMUNICATION.

Anything a company does that influences people (for better or worse) is an act of communication.

It's not just the things the company SAYS that communicate. Everything the corporation and the individuals who represent it do (or don't do), say (or don't say) is something that other people derive meaning from. It's important to remember that PEOPLE CAN BE AS MUCH INFLUENCED BY THINGS THEY MISUNDERSTAND (things the company didn't intend to signal) as by all the carefully crafted press releases and public statements.

CULTURE AND COMMUNICATION

Let's unpack this. Culture thus affects communication in two ways. Firstly, culture underlies the SEMIOTIC RULES we each use to communicate. Semiotics is the system of shared meaning that aids communication between people – even if they don't know one other. To share a system of meaning (what matters, what connects with what) is to share a culture. In other words, CULTURE AND SEMIOTICS ARE TWO SIDES OF THE SAME SHEET OF PAPER. You can flip it over, but you can't split it.

At the most superficial level, this is about language, but it actually goes deeper. The rules of engagement in business are often half-submerged. So, information about how important something is will most often be communicated by referring to 'what everybody knows' – THE CULTURE.

Even the most apparently objective statements are subject to different cultural interpretations. This is the 'lost in translation' effect.

Take a simple phrase like, "This task is the most important activity in the company today." This can be translated between languages accurately, but the meaning depends on the cultural values of the listener. In this case, what matters particularly is the listener's orientation towards time, AND THAT CAN VARY FROM CULTURE TO CULTURE. (I dub this the LOST IN TRANSLATION EFFECT, and it's so pervasive that it applies to other forms of communication too, such as visual communication and the interpretation of actions.)

The second effect of culture on communication revolves around the intent to influence people. Here culture has an effect at a deeper, more unconscious level. When we try to persuade someone of something we may use a number of different strategies. For example:

→ We may choose to list a set of facts and figures that we think point to a particular conclusion.
→ We may choose to talk about the impact on other stakeholders.
→ We may cite previous actions that align with this one.
→ We could even emphasise how the action fits into a holistic system.

Don't be fooled by your instincts. Not everyone looks at things in the same way.

To convince others, we need to find the approach that is most effective in their culture.

We will naturally use the approach that is seen to be most effective within our own culture. But once we step into a CROSS-CULTURAL CONTEXT, using tactics that have always worked at home may just set us up to fail.

It then gets even more complex. Many 'communication episodes' are in fact conversations where people take turns sending and receiving messages. In conversations, MISUNDERSTANDINGS CAN OCCUR IN EACH DIRECTION. This explains how sometimes conversations become unmoored as they spiral upwards, misunderstanding building on new misunderstanding, until grave consequences ensue.

To convince others, we need to find the approach that is most effective in THEIR CULTURE. This statement is not that controversial in the context of a marketing campaign, but as we get further into the business – to internal communication or team management communication – it often attracts resistance.

All too often, the skills involved in cultural awareness or sensitivity are linked to issues around diversity within the organisation, or notions of political correctness, instead of being seen as a responsibility SHARED BY EVERYONE. When conducting business in a cross-cultural environment, if you are not aware of, and sensitive to, the cultures in play, then you are simply making communication choices WITHOUT BEING AWARE OF IT.

If you are not aware of, and sensitive to, the different cultures in play, then you are making communication choices blind.

'Treating everyone the same' means applying cultural values that may just not work. Instead, it's better to make these choices CONSCIOUSLY, IN AN INFORMED WAY. Some choices are hard, involving unavoidable trade-offs. Gains in one sphere will result in losses in another. STRATEGIC THINKING will be required to make the most commercially effective decision.

A WORD ABOUT TOOLS

Cross-cultural study has produced a number of models for measuring and describing the differences between cultures around the world. These generally work by classifying cultures along particular dimensions. I will quote from some of the most famous models, where they throw light on particular issues.

As far as your business is concerned, someone involved in the communications at hand should have at least some familiarity with these tools. How deeply familiar they need to be depends on the exact role and task. You may find it more effective to hire in expertise from the outside for some projects – at which stage my advice is: be wary of someone too invested in a single model. HUMAN CULTURE IS VERY COMPLEX and categorisation can only take you so far.

Globalisation's easy, right? Like the HSBC ads say, just remember not to show the soles of your feet in Thailand and you're halfway there. (If only it were that simple!)

3. CULTURE IN BUSINESS

TIMELINES

There was a day, not so long ago, when globalisation became an everyday fact. Commentators around the world each put a different exact date on it, but some time between 1990 and 2000 the everyday economy went global. Now, we're all trading internationally and, professionally and personally, we benefit from supply chains spanning multiple continents.

The most famous multinationals have been operating around the globe in a modern way for 50 years or more. We all know about it. It's not that hard. Like the HSBC ads say, remember not to show the soles of your feet in Thailand and you're halfway there. AND YET...

As the CEO of a professional services firm recently pointed out to me, his firm is still grappling with the problems culture presents, despite a serious presence abroad since the 1980s. He called the problems, "historic and persistent." Most recently, the firm successfully established new offices in fast-growing parts of the developing world, while a proposed merger with another European firm had fallen through due to a communications breakdown related to different values in the firms' respective cultures.

Cultural problems often make leaders feel inadequate.

In an era of leaky communications, it is less and less possible to present a different corporate face to different cultures.

He also bravely admitted what many business leaders feel, but do not say – CULTURAL PROBLEMS OFTEN MAKE YOU FEEL INADEQUATE AS A LEADER. They spring up unseen from the collective unconscious and are profoundly difficult to get a handle on.

COMMUNICATION LEAKS

Take the more public case of German tyre manufacturer, CONTINENTAL, whose French factory workers pelted managers with eggs, and even occupied a factory, when the firm downsized. The catalyst? The release of plans to Wall Street in an English-language only press release, the day before senior managers were due to address factory employees.

Beyond the obvious offence caused by not translating official statements into the local language, this illustrates a newer problem in cross-cultural communication – one I call THE LAW OF LEAKY COMMUNICATIONS.

This law arises from globalisation and the increasing speed of information spread around the world. It states that it no longer works to address different groups with different communications at different times. Messages pushed through one channel WILL leak out to other audiences, making you look foolish at best, and downright disrespectful at worst.

Some utopians thought globalisation would create a single world culture. Instead, traditional cultural problems remain, and dealing with them has actually become more complex.

CULTURE IN THE INTERNET AGE

Communicating across cultures in business was never simple. The bald advice to 'find the approach that is effective in influencing within the culture of the other party' is the traditional answer (and an important one). But it doesn't tell the whole story. Speed of change, increased globalisation and faster global information flow have caused a NEW SET OF PROBLEMS to emerge. Indeed, contrary to the hopes of some internet/globalisation utopians, TRADITIONAL CULTURAL PROBLEMS REMAIN, exacerbated by two new effects:

→ CULTURES ARE NOT AS CONSTANT A FACTOR AS BEFORE, AND MAP LESS WELL TO SMALLER ENTITIES. Individuals may have been educated, lived and worked in a number of cultures – each one adding a layer to their responses. Groups and individuals may adjust their cultural outlook according to context, particularly distinguishing work from other facets of life.

→ In a more networked world, IT IS LESS AND LESS POSSIBLE TO PRESENT A DIFFERENT CORPORATE (OR INDEED INDIVIDUAL) FACE TO DIFFERENT CULTURES. In an era of leaky communications, people will hear many of the things you say to others and contradictions will be noticed.

Business communications problems and
principles can be grouped into three levels:

→   Global communications
→   Group communications
→   Individual communications

As we go on, we'll talk more about these new problems alongside the traditional ones, putting together principles from both sides to suggest a pragmatic way forward.

A FRAMEWORK FOR UNDERSTANDING BUSINESS COMMUNICATIONS

Business communications covers a wide variety of situations and culture can be an issue in all of them. The problems and principles group into three levels:

→ GLOBAL COMMUNICATIONS – largely about international marketing and branding, but also some aspects of internal communications and corporate conduct within large companies.

→ GROUP COMMUNICATIONS – other aspects of internal communications and the communications within cross-cultural groups.

→ INDIVIDUAL COMMUNICATIONS – beginning with cross-cultural one-to-one conversations and negotiations (a preoccupation for many leaders), but also taking in a few other aspects.

Let's now look at each of these vast topics in turn...

Insisting on consistent international campaigns is self-defeating. Consistency across cultural borders leads to real cross-cultural confusion.

4. COMMUNICATING GLOBALLY (PART ONE) – INTERNATIONAL MARKETING

Two essential dimensions of global communications challenge business leaders. GLOBAL CONDUCT is one, and we'll look at that in the next section. The other is INTERNATIONAL MARKETING.

WHERE THE PROBLEMS BEGIN

A very basic requirement for international marketing is reliable and skilled translation services. The danger is that all too many companies stop there – at most they may tweak a sentence or two, if translators flag up a difficulty. The impulse is to resist FRAGMENTING THE CAMPAIGN – citing either cost pressures or a desire for consistency. This is where the real cross-cultural problems begin.

If international marketing is your responsibility, you'll find more detail in Marieke de Mooij's book (listed in the afterword), which highlights one of the essential dichotomies arising from the logic of modern business – that while DEMAND FOR END PRODUCTS AND SERVICES IS ESSENTIALLY LOCAL (fragmented across the world's diversity of languages, countries and cultures), SUPPLY is generally dominated by the need to achieve ECONOMIES OF SCALE THROUGH STANDARDISATION.

A single name, a single concept, even a single set of communications was the 'holy grail' of global branding in the 1990s. But branding itself is subject to cultural differences.

If your company is only starting out, you may sidestep some of the contradictions inherent in marketing a standard thing across a diverse world by adopting a DIFFERENT PRODUCTION MODEL.

For the rest of us, this is not an immediate option. We are expected to communicate a fairly standard set of company products and services across numerous cultural contexts. As such, the top-level questions are about BRANDING.

The utopian answer in the 1990s was the 'holy grail' of global branding – a single name, a single concept, ideally a single set of communications (perhaps with language translations) all over the world. People expected increasing globalisation to dissolve cultural differences and produce at least a global consumer culture. However, the reality is that the internet age has changed culture only on the surface. In fact, MANY PEOPLE IDENTIFY MORE WITH LOCAL CULTURES THAN BEFORE, so hard choices about cultural difference persist.

EFFECTIVE BRAND ARCHITECTURE ISN'T UNIVERSAL

Fundamentally, BRANDING ITSELF IS SUBJECT TO CULTURE. At this point, like all good management books, it's time to divide the world into two. In this case we'll do it using the dimension of INDIVIDUALISM-COLLECTIVISM from the Hofstede five-dimensional model.

Corporate brands tend to have traction across the world, but product brands only seem to strike a chord where individualism is strong in the culture.

In cultures that show strong individualist values, the notion of an abstract, unique brand personality seems to make sense to consumers (as is the case in the US and Western Europe). However, in collectivist cultures (such as many in Asia) the consumer tends to associate with the company behind the brand. Corporate brands can gain mindshare in both situations, but PRODUCT BRANDS only seem to strike a chord WHERE INDIVIDUALISM IS STRONG.

Of course, while we have this dimension in front of us, you quickly realise that brands that are built on the joys of the INDIVIDUAL life may well struggle in COLLECTIVIST cultures, if they do not find an alternative approach.

EFFECTIVE BRAND IMAGERY IS CULTURE-DEPENDENT

One common technique in advertising, developed in the American (Madison Avenue) model is to associate the product with a 'universal' positive emotion. The trouble is that even these supposedly universal emotions are CONVEYED in very different ways across different cultures.

Take 'success' for example. In Denmark, overt displays are frowned upon, while in Italy, success markers like expensive jewellery are respected and admired.

Madison Avenue-style advertising associates the product with a universally positive emotion. But what evokes that emotion varies from culture to culture.

Hofstede has a dimension that characterises national cultures in terms of nurturing and ambition, which can help marketers to understand how cultures differ with respect to abstract notions like success. It's imperative to realise that the images used to evoke positive associations need to vary when the targeted cultures differ significantly. For maximum cultural effectiveness, a SINGLE CONCEPT should lead to MULTIPLE EXECUTIONS. Those who ignore this fact risk making bad choices about brand imagery.

FACTS, HUMOUR AND COLOUR ALL SIGNIFY DIFFERENTLY

Cultures vary in how much information they use in making a decision. Hall's model measures this in a dimension called HIGH CONTEXT-LOW CONTEXT. In low context cultures, people tend to make decisions on the basis of explicit information – such as product details, or an explanation of the benefits. High context cultures are more likely to consider how the product would fit into an existing situation or social scheme.

At the level of execution, a whole range of topics vary across cultures, from the use of humour, to the symbolic resonance of images, to the associations of various colours. The challenge for the corporation is to make sure that these factual issues are considered, ideally while the strategic brief is still being drawn up. GOOD LOCALISATION ISN'T A BOLT-ON.

The key ingredients of a better approach to international marketing:

→ Culture mapping to show relevant factors and where they come into play

→ Scope and will to decide which facets to present where

→ Feedback loops, so that different views can feed brand concepts

→ Tolerance for polyphony

→ Freedom from iron-clad guidelines that ignore real cultural differences

A BETTER APPROACH TO INTERNATIONAL MARKETING

International corporations have so far adopted a range of options, indicating that there is no single solution. The traditional approach advocated by Marieke de Mooij and others is to adopt AS LOCAL A STRATEGY AS PLAUSIBLE, devolving not only execution, but elements of messaging, and possibly even brand identity, to the level of each cultural cluster you are trading in.

How do you manage this? Many firms have the appropriate brand management structures in place, so all they need to add is some explicit thinking about cultural issues. Broadly, the framework below outlines a sensible, effective approach that moves from CONCEPT to MESSAGING to EXECUTION.

Phase one – brand concept

First, ensure the guardian of the brand identity (the CMO, perhaps?) has an overview of cultural factors that might affect the perception of the company's brand, product and services around the world .

Map how these factors cluster in regions and countries around the world. Use the map to identify where uniform communications may cause frictions, and to decide when and where to adjust them. At the extreme this may involve

Think about cultural differences before agreeing your brand's strategic brief. Good localisation isn't a bolt-on.

splitting a brand along cultural lines, or more often, simply deciding where to present which facets of the brand personality.

This process needs feedback loops between various stages. If a mistake is made in a brand concept, it may be detected only when more local experts get involved. An OPENNESS TO INCORPORATING DIFFERENT VIEWS, an AWARENESS OF AMBIGUITY and a TOLERANCE FOR POLYPHONY in the brand are all critical. Polyphony is a particularly key ingredient because it flies in the face of established brand practice, which is often all about CONTROL – keeping things 'on message' and preventing unauthorised changes.

Phase two – messaging decisions

If messaging is to be outsourced to an agency, those managing the relationship need to be aware of cultural issues and ensure that the agency is dealing with them appropriately. Good decisions need a mix of awareness of cultural values and specific local expertise on the symbols that have currency at the time.

Awareness is all that is needed to link the brand concept with ideas for messages that fit into the target culture. Finely crafting messages for execution, however, requires REAL FAMILIARITY with the language and symbols of the region.

It's crucial that even the local experts have an awareness of cross-cultural translation. This is perhaps the most critical

If messages are too local in scope, they may not cohere with the brand concept. But if they are not local enough they will be too clumsy to succeed.

translation step in the whole exercise. If the 'language and symbols' expert is TOO LOCAL, then they may create messages that work well locally, but do not cohere with the brand concept; NOT LOCAL ENOUGH and the messages they create will appear clumsy.

Phase three – execution

To create copy and artwork that fits into local culture – at the level of values, symbols and fashion – requires people on the team who are in touch with all of these things. Equally, cross-cultural awareness is required to make sure that the local interpretation of values does not become too incoherent with the overall concept.

The process resembles the typical one for turning a brand identity into a communications campaign. The key additions are CROSS-CULTURAL ANALYSIS AND AWARENESS. Some of this can be sourced from the outside, but the awareness needs to reside in INDIVIDUALS WHO MAKE UP THE TEAM. We'll cover how to develop that awareness in the section on individual communications.

A BETTER APPROACH TO INTERNATIONAL MARKETING

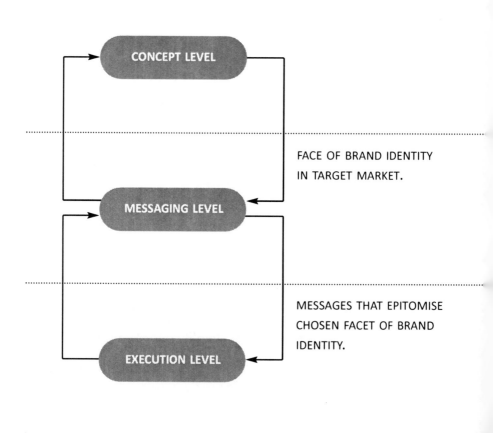

CONCEPT LEVEL

FACE OF BRAND IDENTITY
IN TARGET MARKET.

MESSAGING LEVEL

MESSAGES THAT EPITOMISE
CHOSEN FACET OF BRAND
IDENTITY.

EXECUTION LEVEL

CMO AND TEAM $\longrightarrow$ COMPARE BRAND VALUES WITH NATIONAL VALUES. SEARCH FOR RESONANCES AND CONTRADICTIONS. CHOOSE TO EMPHASISE THOSE THAT SUIT THIS MARKET.

REGIONAL MARKETING TEAM AND AGENCY CREATIVE LEADS $\longrightarrow$ TAKE DESIRED BRAND VALUES AND TRANSLATE THEM INTO IDEAS AND MESSAGES, USING SITUATIONS THAT HAVE MEANING AND RESONANCE IN THE LOCAL MARKET.

COPYWRITERS AND ARTWORKERS $\longrightarrow$ CREATE VISUAL LAYOUTS AND WITTY COPY THAT TELL THE STORY IN FRAMES THAT SPEAK TO THE LOCAL AUDIENCE AT THIS MOMENT IN TIME.

Brands are more than ever in conversation with customers – you need cross-cultural awareness when you listen, as well as when you speak.

DEVOLVING THE PROCESS TO STRENGTHEN THE BRAND

Sharing out responsibility for messaging and execution to strengthen your global brand probably sounds counterintuitive. However, many global branding efforts are stagnating in the face of devolved or local competition. A DEVOLVED PROCESS that allows LOCAL VARIATION looks more effective in this era.

Further, as society changes, brands are more than ever IN CONVERSATION with customers – and so all these structures need to function in BOTH DIRECTIONS. You cannot take the results of a focus group or internet discussion from different cultures and aggregate them without considering the CULTURAL BIASES involved. It's not just about translating language, but also means of expression and assumptions about what is important. Not just symbols, but values too.

Yet the digital age creates the possibility for feedback from cultural groups not targeted initially by a devolved campaign. And smart leaders will want to manage for this as well.

Vodka maker ABSOLUT's recent 'In an Absolut world' campaign in Mexico illustrates just how much the landscape is changing (you'll find a link to the full story in the AFTERWORD). The utopian world it painted – which redrew the map of North America, with Mexico extending far up the West coast of the USA – obviously played well in Mexico but, as the poster

People will see and hear things you say in other cultures. If those messages conflict with those they hear from you in their home country, your reputation will be damaged.

circulated on the internet, it sparked an outcry in the USA, eventually driving the company to issue an official apology.

The point is that the traditional approach to cultural difference – to simply show a different face in different places around the world – is slowly becoming LESS VIABLE. People will see and hear the things you say in other cultures, and if those messages are in conflict with the ones they hear from you in their home country, YOUR REPUTATION WILL BE DAMAGED.

TRUE BRAND COHERENCE AND THE TURN TO AUTHENTICITY

To avoid this damage, your messages will have to become more coherent. Carefully selecting messages used in different cultures will help. So will finding ways to invoke the values of the brand in different places to connect with the different values of the customers, without contradicting the core intention or meaning. The polyphony and tolerance of some ambiguity in branding, mentioned above, remain useful.

But companies more than ever rely on the strength of their brand to radically differentiate themselves from competitors. So companies will evolve a set of brand values that isn't compatible with the entire world. Indeed, the stronger the values of the brand, the more likely it is that it simply won't work in some places. Then we have to make hard choices

Authenticity is the strongest way forward –
for all organisations.

about market and business strategy because TAKING CERTAIN BRANDS TO CERTAIN PLACES IS JUST A WASTE OF EFFORT.

Large multinationals, like PROCTOR AND GAMBLE or UNILEVER, may not find this too onerous, given they maintain a large stable of brands. Smaller organisations, however, face a trade-off between altering their values to suit their most profitable markets or retaining their identity. Culture-clash denies them success in some parts of the world.

My own belief is that AUTHENTICITY is the strongest way forward – FOR ALL ORGANISATIONS. The internal contradictions of presenting a number of faces to the world will slowly eat at the competitive advantage of those who try have a number of identities – both due to attacks from other brands on the outside, and the dissonance it creates amongst employees dealing within an incoherent employer brand. As such, it looks like AUTHENTICITY IS THE ONLY TRULY SUSTAINABLE, LONG-TERM APPROACH.

In the short-term, it may be painful to let go of some possible markets because they are not compatible with your brand culture, but the pay-off is that it ALLOWS YOUR OWN VALUES TO BE THE COMPASS FOR YOUR ORGANISATION – which is vital part of success in an ever more complex world.

The culture of the observer determines whether any particular local action is seen as good or bad. Don't override your instinctive answer when it doesn't match local customs.

Instead, stop and think.

5. COMMUNICATING GLOBALLY (PART TWO) – GLOBAL CONDUCT

No discussion that arrives at authenticity as a strategic mandate can avoid the theme of GLOBAL CONDUCT.

Some of the most common questions raised are those of ETHICS. Notably, two areas are hot topics at the moment: CORRUPTION and ENVIRONMENTAL RESPONSIBILITY. Corruption is a recurring topic, and sets a framework that is helpful for thinking about environmental issues, too.

The status of any particular act is often open to interpretation through the lens of culture. Is something a bribe, or a small commission fee? Are extra payments to the brother of the CEO of the customer firm a kind of referral fee, badly monitored consulting fees, or nepotism and corrupt malpractice?

Assuming that you are in a part of the world where the law does not provide a clear 'don't do it', the answer depends in part on the local culture. If your instinctive answer does not match local customs you certainly have some thinking to do.

Part of being prepared for cross-cultural situations is having a clear sense of one's own values.

Things to consider:

→ WHAT ARE YOUR (CORPORATE/PERSONAL) VALUES?

Many practices occur around the world, but trading in those places does not mean one must bend to them. AUTHENTICITY IS KEY. Part of being prepared for cross-cultural situations is having a CLEAR SENSE OF ONE'S OWN VALUES – the things that are acceptable to you and the things that are not. What kinds of actions are not in line with your values? You have to know CONSCIOUSLY WHAT WILL CAUSE YOU TO WALK AWAY from a contract.

→ DO YOU DO IMPORTANT BUSINESS IN A MARKET WHERE THERE ARE LEGAL PROVISIONS TO PROSECUTE CORRUPTION IN FOREIGN CONTRACTS?

BRITISH AEROSPACE is a recent example of a firm who incurred heavy fines in the USA for ambiguous payments on contracts in other parts of the world.

→ ARE THERE REPUTATION EFFECTS IN IMPORTANT MARKETS THAT MIGHT BE AS DAMAGING AS THE LEGAL EFFECTS ABOVE?

You may not always incur fines, but you may lose business if revelations about your activities damage your reputation.

Conducting business across cultural borders leads smart businesses to a clearer, more coherent sense of what their brand is, means and does.

This approach applies quite well to environmental matters, too. There are a number of cultures where neither the natural world nor the state of the global environment is currently a strong consideration. You may be asked to be party to environmentally damaging actions as part of a contract. By assessing your values in advance, deciding what you can authentically sign up to, and what you will walk away from, you will be able to make the choice consciously, and explain your decision to others.

Overall, as with branding, conducting business across not simply national – but also CULTURAL – borders leads smart businesses to a CLEARER, MORE COHERENT, MORE ANCHORED SENSE OF WHAT THEIR BRAND IS, MEANS AND DOES. Decisions about formal communications – like branded advertising – and about official or unofficial conduct need to flow from this authentic sense and not undermine it. This can imply some limitations. Some businesses won't expand into all geographies and may withdraw from cultures where their values don't sync, but AUTHENTIC BRANDS WILL FIND IT EASIER TO MAKE MEANINGFUL PROMISES they can fulfil in practice.

Employees may self-select to work for a foreign firm in order to get away from aspects of local culture that do not suit them.

6. GROUP COMMUNICATIONS

When we talk about communicating with groups, a number of things are distinct from the global case. These also apply to targeted marketing communications within a country, but (for brevity) this section will concentrate on the case of INTERNAL COMMUNICATIONS within a multi-national corporation.

ALL GROUPS HAVE A CULTURE OF THEIR OWN...

Group culture is never only a reflection of national culture. It depends as well on the kind of people recruited and the corporate culture.

Recently, the Indian division of a US bank was sold to a Japanese bank. It was thought that the Indians would find the more collective culture of the Japanese bank more comfortable than the strongly individualist values of the US bank.

However, the overriding concern for the employees was the worry that the Japanese bank would change the individual bonus structure! These employees had SELF-SELECTED to join the US bank because they wanted to work in an environment LESS COLLECTIVIST THAN THEIR NATIONAL INDIAN CULTURE.

The entire company may talk in the same jargon and use the same slogans, but the meaning of the words will vary from place to place.

...BUT CULTURAL DIFFERENCES PERSIST

Corporations develop a language all of their own and phrases like 'customer first' are a common shorthand. They often crop up when strategy is being communicated across the business. It is very dangerous to assume that everyone automatically understands the same thing from these phrases.

This is not just a question of translation in language, but also of translation of CULTURAL PRIORITY. Notably, in cultures where a great deal of respect is paid to hierarchical status, it can be very difficult for an employee to put the CUSTOMER ahead of the stated wishes of their SUPERIOR. Yet, when asked, they will definitely say that 'in this company, we put the customer first'.

There are really two points here:

→ What people SAY THEY BELIEVE and what their behaviours SHOW THEM TO BELIEVE can diverge.

→ When diverse groups all SAY the same thing, they can mean DIFFERENT THINGS WITH THE SAME WORDS. This is because we speak with words, but it is ideas and beliefs (not phrases) that shape our actions.

Improving cross-cultural information flows is a vital task for the modern internal communicator.

Working successfully across cultures means becoming aware of these two dynamics. They come into play any time alignment of cross-cultural teams (or teams across cultures) is the aim.

MULTI-NATIONALS — A CONSTELLATION OF GROUPS

A corporate group (in this case a multi-national) is in fact a constellation of groups, all of which interact. This has two major impacts:

First, while the first reaction may be simply to target communications to each culture separately, information transfer between groups means that great care must be taken over the COHERENCE OF MESSAGES. If the messages sent out in different cultures conflict, then credibility can be fatally damaged.

Second, communication between groups is a major area of confusion rooted in cultural difference. A vital task for the cross-culturally aware communicator is helping to improve these CROSS-CULTURAL INFORMATION FLOWS.

Thus, the challenges in group communication may be divided into two areas — MESSAGING and FACILITATION.

Reasons communicators broadcast messages to the whole organisation include:

→ Informing people about corporate strategy and values.

→ Motivating behaviour that is in alignment with the goals of the organisation.

→ Keeping people informed of changes that they might otherwise not hear about.

'MESSAGING' IN THE GROUP CONTEXT

A common challenge for communicators is to convey information about strategy and change to everyone in the corporate body. Translating the abstract into 'what does it mean to me' is key, and this can be a very culturally sensitive step. The first step is to map out the cultures present in the organisation and (in larger organisations) cluster them into a practical number of groups.

If the corporate culture is strong, and the contacts between groups are high, SEGMENTING MESSAGE STRATEGIES IS A WASTE OF EFFORT. The benefits of presenting different faces to different audiences will be offset by the frictions when they discover inconsistencies between presentations in different parts of the world. However, it is still vital to think about whether language translation is needed (and cultural concept translation), and to consider different communication and information processing styles.

In cases where you have offices or Divisions with very distinct cultures, then it's more important to consider targeting DIFFERENT MESSAGES, concentrating on DIFFERENT VALUES to those offices. As in the global case, a structure should be devised that ensures some level of coherence between messages – otherwise you may create as many frictions as you solve.

Assess the strength of corporate culture and map the national cultures involved before adjusting your communications.

Always remember that global business standards fit more effectively into some cultures than others. When communicating about new HR schemes in particular, it is very important to realise that different cultures will evaluate the schemes very differently.

The Trompenaars/Hampden-Turner model has a dimension that runs from UNIVERSALIST TO PARTICULARIST, indicating whether a culture considers it more just for rules to be applied in the same way to everyone (universalist), or to be modified according to situation and context (particularist). The economic logic of global business pushes towards HR solutions that fit universalist cultures. Depending on the geographical spread of your business, this may provoke an UNRESOLVABLE CONTRADICTION. If you are split 50/50 across universalist and particularist cultures, then it is very difficult to create a policy that works well everywhere. Communication cannot solve this contradiction, but there is great value in NOT MAKING THINGS WORSE by assuming everyone will welcome your chosen policy.

To sum up, it's important to assess the strength of corporate culture and map the national cultures involved before deciding how much to adjust the 'values presentation' of communications in each country. Adjusting for different information processing styles and language should be considered in every case.

No culture is happy to be 'last to know.' It's vital to ensure that messages arrive at the same time, otherwise trust will collapse.

Finally, as the earlier case involving CONTINENTAL reminds us, NO CULTURE IS HAPPY TO BE 'LAST TO KNOW'. Even if you are communicating varied messages to different groups, they must still receive the information AT THE SAME TIME, otherwise the messages that arrive late will be treated with suspicion.

FACILITATING INTER-GROUP COMMUNICATION

Communicators are often asked to recommend translation services when communication between groups is going wrong.

However, very often the problem is not at the level of language, but AT THE LEVEL OF CULTURE. It's easy for different groups in a company to assume that 'we all think the same way', but this is rarely the case. Culture affects the way we process and express information, perceive meanings and allocate priorities.

Cross-cultural awareness allows one to spot that it is culture (rather than other possible causes – e.g. bad incentives, political power plays) causing communication problems between groups. Fixing it involves working to raise the cross-cultural skills of key participants in communication loops – typically this may involve education about different aspects of cultural values, training about the specific values in play and group workshops involving all participants to build new understandings.

It's more important to focus on signs of potential misunderstanding than to apply pre-determined assumptions about how the conversation will proceed.

7. INDIVIDUAL COMMUNICATIONS

No individual communication is entirely culturally determined. Our conversations are the outcome of the combination of CULTURE, INDIVIDUAL PSYCHOLOGY and the CONTEXT OF THE SITUATION.

However, it is often the case in international business that misunderstandings arise from cultural differences. This can be because both parties use the same words, but they have different cultural meanings; or because we assume both parties have the same motivations, but in fact people from different cultures often approach situations with different goals.

Perhaps the most obvious example is to do with SHORT-TERM VERSUS LONG-TERM THINKING. Business culture in the Anglo-American world is renowned for a 'quarter by quarter' approach, but some cultures emphasise a longer time scale for measuring results. However, an extra caveat is necessary.

It's no longer as useful as before to stereotype the people you interact with. They may have lived and worked in a number of countries. Such a range of influences means that it is often more important to focus on SIGNS OF POTENTIAL MISUNDERSTANDING, than to apply a pre-packed set of assumptions about how the interaction will proceed.

Checklists about manners and body language are useful, but they do not address the problems that deep culture poses.

CROSS-CULTURAL CONVERSATIONS

We make a distinction between conversations and negotiations because negotiations involve an extra level of complexity.

Some say that meaningful cross-cultural understanding is impossible unless both parties speak the language of the other. It is certainly true that 'speaking their language' can improve mutual understanding. Despite this, the reality of modern business is that a senior manager will have to engage with partners from all around the world. Sooner or later, you will encounter a situation beyond your personal language skills. The commercial imperative requires that you proceed and

AN UNDERSTANDING OF CULTURE IS THE BEST GUIDE TO REDUCING CONFUSION.

Many companies offer web resources and short courses that focus on the superficial aspects of cross-cultural encounters. They will tell you, for example, that one should not show the soles of your feet in Thailand and that, in the USA, people prefer a greater degree of personal space than elsewhere.

These checklists of faux-pas to avoid are not useless. Little signals that you have attempted to understand your opposite number can be to your credit. However, THEY DO NOT ADD UP TO CROSS-CULTURAL AWARENESS AND DO NOT ADDRESS THE PROBLEMS DEEP CULTURE POSES.

When two partners get a year into a joint venture before they discover they entered the agreement with different purposes, it isn't because one of them forgot to shake hands when they first met.

Further, as business internationalises, people are less and less concerned by minor mistakes in matters of courtesy from foreigners. More and more people understand that we cannot expect outsiders to be 'just like us'. A checklist of mistakes can inspire anxiety and distract us from noticing the CULTURAL AND COMMERCIAL UNDERCURRENTS in front of us. At worst (as we'll see in the negotiation section), it creates a mindset that gives away too much power in the name of cross-cultural sensitivity.

The critical first step to successful conversation in cross-cultural situations is an AWARENESS OF YOUR OWN CULTURAL BACKGROUND. It is only by becoming conscious of the expectations you have about how communication works that you will become able to navigate a conversation with someone who is working to a different cultural 'programme'. This self-awareness should include at least:

→ AN IDEA OF WHICH CULTURE (IF YOU HAVE A VARIED BACKGROUND) HAS THE MOST INFLUENCE ON YOU.

→ A SENSE OF THE UNDERLYING VALUES OF THAT 'HOME' CULTURE USING ONE OF THE MAJOR MODELS, SUCH AS HOFSTEDE. (You need a major model to give you the confidence and evidence backing to be able to then make comparisons with other cultures.)

Awareness of your own cultural background is critical. Successfully navigating cross-cultural conversations begins with self-knowledge.

→ AN IDEA OF THE PREFERRED COMMUNICATION STYLE IN YOUR CULTURE, WITH PARTICULAR ATTENTION TO WHETHER IT IS HIGH OR LOW CONTEXT, including a sense of what kind of persuasion approaches are accorded most status in the culture, and specific ways that agreement, disagreement, comfort and discomfort are expressed.

→ A SENSE OF THE RELATIONSHIP BETWEEN YOUR OWN PERSONALITY AND THE CULTURE. Do you find it all makes sense, or have you always felt that (in various ways) you don't quite fit the stereotype?

Only with SELF-KNOWLEDGE can you be prepared to navigate conversations and minimise the misunderstandings that result from deeper culture.

In the simplest situations, you may interact with someone whose background is firmly rooted in their home country culture. Here, you can undertake looking into the first three points in the list above for that culture. By comparing the other's culture to your own, you gain a sense of where misunderstandings may occur. What you cannot know until you meet the person and start talking with them is anything about the fourth question – THEIR RELATIONSHIP WITH THEIR OWN CULTURE.

Be mindful that this meeting is not just another meeting like those you go to every Monday back at HQ. You may not get the expected responses to your signals.

What should be apparent already from this point is that, even in this relatively simple scenario, FACTS AND KNOWLEDGE CAN ONLY TAKE YOU SO FAR. The purpose of assembling these questions is to remind you to be mindful. Be mindful that:

→ Things in this meeting do not work exactly like the Monday morning meeting back at HQ every week.

→ You may not get the expected responses when you send out signals, especially about inquiries into sensitive topics.

→ The person across the table may not be driven to seek the same outcomes as you.

The saving grace of a friendly conversation is that one can actually inquire into the state of mind of the other person. Of course, how they express themselves will come through the filter of their culture, but it is possible to enlist them in helping you make sense of the conversation.

What should be clear is that this is not something you can just do 'by the book' — it is a skill of noticing reactions and CONSCIOUSLY INTERPRETING THEM, aware that your instinctive perception may not be accurate.

Fixing culture problems is all about developing cross-cultural skills – part knowledge, part practice.

It all becomes even more complicated with today's 'global nomads' who are part of many international businesses. They will likely have a 'home' culture, but it may not be the one you would guess from their CV. At this point, you can no longer even look up their cultural style in a book beforehand, BECAUSE YOU DON'T KNOW WHAT IT IS. (Fortunately, such nomads are unlikely to be worried about the superficial mistakes.)

So how do you develop a cultural awareness that you can use it in real time? We'll address that in the next chapter, but first some words on negotiations...

CROSS-CULTURAL NEGOTIATIONS

Negotiations add an extra layer of complexity. If cross-cultural conversation is about clarity, then in negotiation you often want to OBSCURE YOUR POSITION (your exact aims, your weaknesses) in order to gain an advantage.

To some degree one can use the techniques of cross-cultural conversation to understand the signals being sent and make sure you send back ones that accurately represent your negotiating position. However, you have to be aware of the pitfall that 'cultural awareness' can represent.

It's not uncommon for the eagerness to show cultural sensitivity can be taken advantage of, as in the case of extended

If you are not competent at cross-cultural conversation, then cross-cultural negotiation is like trying to paint a portrait with a blindfold on!

negotiations between a European parts supplier and Middle Eastern oil company. Anxious not to upset the customer by being 'too Western' and forcing the pace, it eventually became clear to the supplier that the oil company had used their protracted negotiations as a bargaining tool to get a better deal with another supplier. The supplier's desire not to be culturally insensitive or 'foreign' had allowed it to be used for other purposes.

You can use the techniques of cross-cultural conversation to ensure that you understand the signals you are receiving and to ensure that the ones you send accurately portray your position. However, you must always consider the commercial logic of your position and the negotiation. Sometimes you have to know WHEN to "be foreign", or else you may find your cross-cultural awareness is used against you.

This is something you can only pick up by experience. There is no way that cross-cultural negotiation will ever be easy. It will always be an art. But, if you are not competent at cross-cultural conversation, cross-cultural negotiation is like trying to paint a portrait with a blindfold on!

At the very least, leadership needs to be cross-culturally aware. If you don't know what culture is, and how it can affect the way brands are expressed and experienced, then you're in trouble.

8. CONCLUSIONS – THE ONGOING JOURNEY FROM AWARENESS TO COMPETENCE

A running theme through this book has been the need for more people in the organisation to become CROSS-CULTURALLY AWARE. However, not everyone needs to know the same things, so here we break the knowledge down into roles that fit into the different kinds of communication described, and into two different skill levels – AWARENESS and COMPETENCE. This is accompanied by comments on how to acquire the skills or source the expertise involved.

AT THE GLOBAL COMMUNICATION LEVEL

At the top level, leaders need at the very least to be cross-culturally aware, with a particular focus on THE INTERACTION OF CULTURE WITH PRODUCTS AND BRANDS. Awareness in this case involves familiarity with:

→ What culture is.
→ How the differences between cultures can be modelled.
→ A framework relating those measured cultural values to the way brands and brand values are expressed, in order to spot potential problems.

Leaders need to know enough to take informed decisions about how to resolve the problems culture can present.

Detailed analysis in this area can be sourced from consultants, but LEADERS NEED TO KNOW ENOUGH TO TAKE INFORMED DECISIONS. This knowledge can be gained through independent reading, but short courses are also available.

At the level of messaging, general awareness should be supplemented by people with experience in the PRACTICE of cross-cultural communication (as opposed to the STRATEGY). This typically means individuals well on the road to cross-cultural competence. Experience running international campaigns is always valuable, but does not always in itself indicate cross-cultural competence.

To bridge messaging and execution requires someone cross-culturally competent and WITH KNOWLEDGE OF THE SPECIFIC CULTURES INVOLVED. This is where agencies and consultants come into play, because few companies have all the necessary knowledge in-house.

Similarly for execution, knowledge of local culture, language, and symbols, such as fashions and visual expression, are vital. This range of knowledge is most often found in the region in question. However the team needs at least one bridge member who is aware of cross-cultural issues and CAN TRANSLATE NOT ONLY LANGUAGE, BUT ALSO CULTURAL CONCEPTS. Otherwise the hard work of earlier stages may be lost.

Not every group communication problem is rooted in culture-clash – but you need a high degree of cross-cultural competence to know whether or not culture is the problem.

AT THE GROUP COMMUNICATION LEVEL

For group communications, a similar mix to the global communications setup is ideal. At the same time, internal communications budgets are typically more stretched. The simplest approach in such cases is to cut back on local specialists. This approach in turn creates a stronger imperative that those who remain are CROSS-CULTURALLY COMPETENT rather than just aware, as they will be required to operate across several cultures.

For FACILITATION OF GROUP-TO-GROUP COMMUNICATION, a high degree of cross-cultural competence is required. Not only does the role call for diagnosing whether communications problems have cultural or other roots, but the solution involves RAISING THE CULTURAL AWARENESS OF OTHERS. Many organisations find it most effective to have a cross-culturally competent 'trouble spotter' who then sources deep diagnosis and problem-solving from outside experts.

AT THE INDIVIDUAL COMMUNICATION LEVEL

We've talked about being cross-culturally aware in the BRAND context, and this is part of the story in the individual context too. However, as outlined earlier, it is vital for individuals to develop SELF-AWARENESS in the cultural sphere too.

This is where you need to answer the questions on pages 73-77. It is possible to do this mostly on your own, but AN OUTSIDE

Global experience, book learning and behavioural work are all equally important in developing cross-cultural competence.

VIEWPOINT IS ESSENTIAL FOR THE DEVELOPMENT OF AN ACCURATE SELF-PORTRAIT. Discussions with a cross-cultural expert can highlight subtleties that you will miss when working alone from books.

This higher degree of cross-cultural awareness begins the road to cross-cultural competence. In taking yourself on this journey, the GLOBAL MINDSET INVENTORY (presented by Javidan-Teagarden & Bowen) is a good guide to self-directed learning. In particular, the division of the list into areas of INTELLECTUAL, PSYCHOLOGICAL and SOCIAL capital are a great reminder that global experience, book-learning and behavioural work are all EQUALLY IMPORTANT in developing cross-cultural competence.

Beyond your own activities, training about specific cultures certainly helps. Every new culture encountered raises the mindfulness of how cultural difference can be experienced. As noted in the section on CROSS-CULTURAL CONVERSATIONS, there are many times when a short study of a particular culture can aid achieving business objectives.

Much rarer, but more important is a CROSS-CULTURAL DEBRIEF following a cross-cultural assignment or encounter. Theory in advance helps prepare the mind, but it is REFLECTION ON REAL EVENTS THAT TURNS THEM INTO 'EXPERIENCE'. This should be standard practice, but too often people think 'it's over now, why think about it?'

Cross-cultural competence means gaining a bone-deep understanding that there is more than one way to perceive, interpret and act in the world.

Some cross-culturalists provide simulations of cross-cultural encounters, either in the form of educational videos or advanced role-play sessions. These are a useful, safe space to practice MINDFULNESS, observing the different ways people communicate and react and monitoring their own instinctive interpretations.

While theory and simulation are both necesssary and useful, THERE IS NO SUBSTITUTE FOR EXPERIENCE. Living and working in another culture brings a deep understanding that there is more than one way to perceive, interpret and act in the world. It is that BONE-DEEP UNDERSTANDING, that CROSS-CULTURAL MUSCLE MEMORY that marks out the truly cross-culturally competent.

Authenticity and mindfulness are at the centre of success in a cross-cultural context.

IN PARTING

I hope this book does three things:

→ Inspires you to make cross-cultural understanding part of how you conduct business communications.

→ Provides you with useful ideas for how to make that happen.

→ Alerts you to the future of cross-cultural communications in our globalised world.

If you only learn and work with two ideas, let them be these:

→ AUTHENTICITY, BASED ON SELF-KNOWLEDGE, is the centrepiece of a successful cross-cultural attitude at both the corporate and personal levels.

→ MINDFULNESS OF BOTH YOUR OWN GOALS AND THE MULTIPLE MEANINGS COMMUNICATIONS MAY HAVE is at the heart of successful cross-cultural interchange.

9. GLOSSARY OF TERMS

AUTHENTICITY – acting in ways that match your values; requires knowing what your values are and paying attention to any gaps between 'values statements' and what you really believe.

BEHAVIOUR – actions and reactions in the world, sometimes conscious, sometimes unconscious. Individual behaviour is prompted by a combination of CULTURE and INDIVIDUAL TRAITS (see below), combined with the context of the moment. Many people prefer to believe that individual behaviour is a pure reflection of individual traits, unaffected by others (culture) or surroundings (context). Alas, the evidence is against them!

BUSINESS COMMUNICATION – communication undertaken to influence the choices of others, for commercial purposes.

COHERENCE – the quality of unity, even if messages aren't exactly the same. Absolute consistency (the same message all around the world) simply doesn't do the job, because different groups receive different meanings from the same message. Coherence is a much more important aim in the context of cross-cultural communications – i.e. different expressions that are mutually supportive and do not contradict each other.

COMMUNICATION – a process whereby information is transferred from one entity to another. In order to effect the transfer, at least two agents are involved, the proverbial 'sender' and 'receiver'. Critically, communication is not just a question of intentional signals. The other party may find meaning in every action and every choice not to act.

CROSS-CULTURAL – involving people or groups from one or more cultures. INTERCULTURAL (see below) is also often used to mean the same thing.

CROSS-CULTURAL ANALYSIS – examination of how the deep values of culture(s) impact on the issue at hand.

CROSS-CULTURAL AWARENESS – an awareness that different cultures have different values and, conseqeuently, that communications and actions will be perceived differently by different groups. Allowing one to spot the potential for culture (rather than other possible causes) to be the cause of communication problems, it should be a basic requirement in international business. Too often it isn't.

CROSS-CULTURAL CONVERSATIONS – conversations involving people or groups from one or more cultures (obvious, right?!). The problem lies in the fact that communication goes back and forth a number of times, which means that small errors of perception can create a feedback loop until the two parties are talking about completely different things. A huge area for potential misunderstandings, yet many corporations pay no attention to improving them.

CULTURE – effectively the collective unconscious of a group ('The way we do things around here'). A set of norms about BEHAVIOUR (see above) and the meaning of events that influences choices and actions. It's not the only thing governing actions and behaviour, but it's often the most underestimated element.

CULTURE-CLASH – a set of misunderstandings, conflicts or disagreements arising from the differences in deep, unconscious values of people from different cultures.

DIVERSITY – an important concept in creating high-performing teams that do not lapse into groupthink or complacency. Diversity is about including people from different cultures in decisions and operations. However, the term has largely been appropriated by HR practitioners who have given it a bad name amongst businesses – associating it with various levels of political correctness.

FACILITATION – an entirely underrated activity in many communications frameworks. Facilitators enable different groups to engage with each other, improving their mutual understanding and helping them achieve more.

FAST AND SLOW CULTURE – Grant McCracken's framework for how to think about the connection between fads and fashions and deeper cultural trends and values. Further explanation here: www.throughline.co.uk/2010/10/28/the-elements-of-culture

GLOBALISATION – the increasing level of connection between people, systems and businesses across the world.

GLOBAL BRANDING – the utopian school of thought that believes the future of brands is consistency across the planet, with no concessions to location or culture.

INDIVIDUAL TRAITS – the elements of personality or character that describe how individuals typically react to a situation.

INTERCULTURAL – commonly used to mean the same as CROSS-CULTURAL (see above), although some writers distinguish between the two terms in various ways (e.g. INTERCULTURAL as dealing with interactions, and CROSS-CULTURAL as about comparisons.)

INTERNATIONAL CULTURE – in this book, the question of cultures found in different geographic regions of the world, in contrast to ORGANISATIONAL CULTURE (see below). This edition concentrates on international culture as it remains the place where businesspeople most often realise they encounter problems.

LAW OF LEAKY COMMUNICATIONS – the tendency of communications in the modern age to spread beyond their first recipients, often due to the ease of sharing and translating that digital technology brings to the world.

LOST IN TRANSLATION EFFECT – the same phrase invoking different reactions in different cultures, even when perfectly translated, because different cultures have different senses of what is important with respect to time, hierarchy and society.

MESSAGING – used in this book to talk about the 'broadcast' communication undertaken in many organisations from central offices to teams around the world.

ORGANISATIONAL CULTURE – the culture of groups defined by their organisational home. This exists both at the macro-level (e.g. company) and micro-level (e.g. department). Many of the principles of cross-cultural communication in this book are described with respect to international culture, but apply to organisational culture too.

POLYPHONY – Speech composed of a diversity of points of view and voices. The last 30 years of corporate communications have been fiercely concentrated on control, keeping things 'consistent', speaking with 'one voice'. This is impossible in a cross-cultural context. Polyphony needs to be embraced and consistency replaced with COHERENCE (see above).

SEMIOTICS – the shared system of meaning that glues people of the same culture together. Also, the study of how meaning is created and exchanged in culture.

SEMIOTIC RULES – a rule-based description of how meaning arises in a culture that takes into account what the culture determines as valuable, the visual and verbal language typical of the culture.

10. AFTERWORD

In the long line of prominent cross-cultural experts from the Netherlands, MIJND HUISER is not one of the most famous. Indeed, while his published work and 'Model of Freedom' are useful and interesting, they didn't make it into the main part of this book. However, I have to credit him with inspiring me to write about authenticity. At a public lecture he gave, he responded to a question about corruption with a very clear articulation of authenticity as the way forward. The exact words passed from my memory years ago, but the sense that the purpose of cross-cultural awareness is to allow us to make authentic decisions remained.

Thanks are due to many people for making this book possible, but a few deserve a special mention. KEVIN KEOHANE and DAN GRAY for inviting me to write on the subject and sticking with me through some difficult times. And my business partner, KATE HAMMER, a commercial storyteller, for the ongoing conversation about culture in business.

If your interest in cross-cultural issues has been stimulated, please join in the discussions on the THROUGHLINE BLOG (http://www.throughline.co.uk/water-cooler) or find me on Twitter (@Indy_Neogy).

In addition, here are some books and articles that you may find useful:

BEYOND CULTURE — EDWARD T. HALL

CHIEF CULTURE OFFICER — GRANT MCCRACKEN

THE CULTURAL ADVANTAGE — MIJND HUIJSER

CULTURES AND ORGANIZATIONS: SOFTWARE FOR THE MIND — GEERT HOFSTEDE

GLOBAL MARKETING AND ADVERTISING: UNDERSTANDING CULTURAL PARADOXES — MARIEKE DE MOOIJ

THE INTERPRETATION OF CULTURES — CLIFFORD GEERTZ

MANAGING YOURSELF: MAKING IT OVERSEAS — JAVIDAN, TEAGARDEN & BOWEN (HARVARD BUSINESS REVIEW, APRIL 2010)

RIDING THE WAVES OF CULTURE: UNDERSTANDING CULTURAL DIVERSITY IN BUSINESS — FONS TROMPENAARS & CHARLES HAMPDEN-TURNER

ABSOLUT VODKA PULLS AD SHOWING CALIFORNIA IN MEXICO — HTTP://WWW.REUTERS.COM/ARTICLE/IDUSN0729018920080409

MEXICO RECONQUERS CALIFORNIA? ABSOLUT DRINKS TO THAT! — HTTP://LATIMESBLOGS.LATIMES.COM/LAPLAZA/2008/04/MEXICO-RECONQUE.HTML

ABOUT THE AUTHOR

INDY NEOGY is a business consultant who has spent the last decade finding solutions to the problems culture poses for commerce. His career has covered six business sectors, seven countries and three continents.

After school in England, he studied at MIT, earning a combined degree in Aerospace Engineering and Media Studies. After several interesting years, taking in everything from pioneering new photographic techniques for motion capture in the UK to joining a groundbreaking internet media streaming team in the Netherlands, Indy decided it was time to refocus on the problems of culture in business. He completed an MBA at the University of Leeds and published on co-operation between groups in health services across Europe, going on to develop an independent practice in cross-cultural consulting, with an emphasis on the financial services, energy and professional services sectors.

Indy currently heads up the culture and innovation practice at THROUGHLINE, a boutique consultancy that solves business problems using the power of conversations, stories and culture. He is also one of the founders of KILN – a company that kick-starts corporate innovation using trend intelligence.

In his spare time he remains a keen photographer, voracious culture scanner and is a Fellow of the Royal Society for the Arts.

You can reach him at indy@throughline.co.uk, via the blog (www.throughline.co.uk/water-cooler/) or through LinkedIn and Twitter (@Indy_Neogy).

Far too many business books start with the false premise that offering meaningful insight requires exhaustive detail. They demand a huge investment from readers to wade through all the information provided and draw out what is relevant to them.

In a rapidly changing, time-starved world, it's an approach that's getting wronger and wronger. What CEOs and other busy business people desperately need is high-level strategic insight delivered in quick, simple, easy-to-digest packages.

Co-created by KEVIN KEOHANE AND DAN GRAY, that's exactly what the 55-MINUTE GUIDES are designed to do. Instead of some 300-page pseudo-academic tome, they offer fresh perspectives and 'must knows' on important topics that can be read from cover to cover in the course of a single morning's commute or a short plane ride.

In short, they are the antidote to most business books. A QUICK READ, not a long slog. Focused on BIG IDEAS, not technical detail. Promoting JOINED-UP THINKING, not functional bias. Written to EMPOWER THE READER, not to make the author look clever.

They're guided by the simple principle that INSIGHT GAINED PER MINUTE SPENT READING should be as high as possible. No fluff. No filler. No jargon. Just the things you REALLY need to know, written in plain English with clear and simple illustrations.

Lightning Source UK Ltd.
Milton Keynes UK
UKOW040254180712

196163UK00005B/18/P